You're the
Best Sister Ever

You're the

Best Sister Ever

Maria Smedstad

Andrews McMeel
Publishing
Kansas City

ISBN: 0-7407-3856-9

Library of Congress Control Number: 2003102702

03 04 05 06 07 WKT 10 9 8 7 6 5 4 3 2 1

Introduction

My parents are under the impression that it was my sister, Hanna (older than me by three years), who taught me how to read, write, tie my shoelaces, and tell the time. They are wrong. It is true that Hanna *attempted* to teach me things with the best of intentions in mind. However, as I continued to stare at her beautifully made demonstrative cardboard clock in complete incomprehension, these occasions were usually cut short by her shouting at me, throwing the mock clock out the window, and kicking me in the leg. Not that I didn't learn from this. I came to realize that in order to keep things sweet I needed to learn how to work those numbers and letters *before* she attempted to teach them to me, so that it could appear as though she were doing a good job.

You see, I had come to the conclusion that a sister is a pretty good thing to have on your side. Not only does she have good taste in comics and hair bands, she also makes a very good friend. And this is, in my mind, what makes a sister so special. She is the one person who will never go away, no matter how far apart you live. You can even forget her birthday (not too often, though) and she will still remember yours. She knows you like no one else, because she was there growing up alongside you. Nothing else compares to that. I know now just how lucky I am to have a sister like Hanna (despite her nearly scalping me with her early French-braiding attempts).

Chances are, if you have received this book, you are a fairly lucky sister, too.

I can phone you at
four in the morning,
and it won't matter.

You know what I wear
(and what I eat)
when I think no one else
is around, and you still
seem to love me.

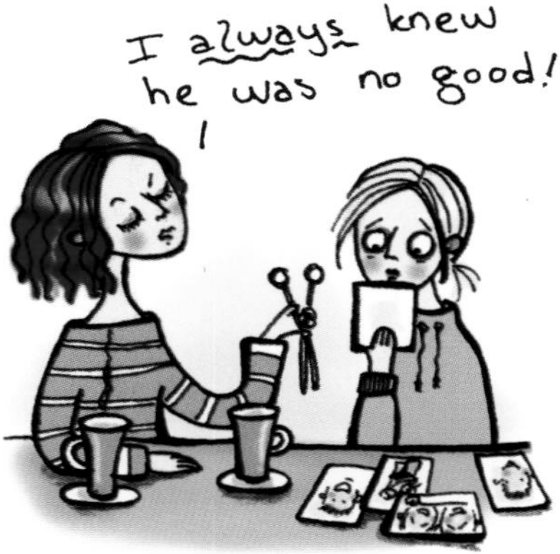
I always knew he was no good!

You love my friends but dislike
my enemies more than I do.

We communicate perfectly
without words.

You talk to our parents
on my behalf when
we are "not talking."

... mom, you should see what the poor thing is reduced to wearing nowadays!!

You also talk to our parents
when I am broke but
too proud to say so.

You never say "I told you so."

I don't have to explain to you where I'm from, because you were always there with me.

You teach my boyfriends
a thing or two.

You hold the hair from my face when I'm being sick.

You supply me with a very nice
second wardrobe . . .

not to mention other freebies!

You're the first to help me
redecorate when I move.

We share the same irrational phobias, brought on by childhood family traumas.

I can rely on your
honest opinion . . .

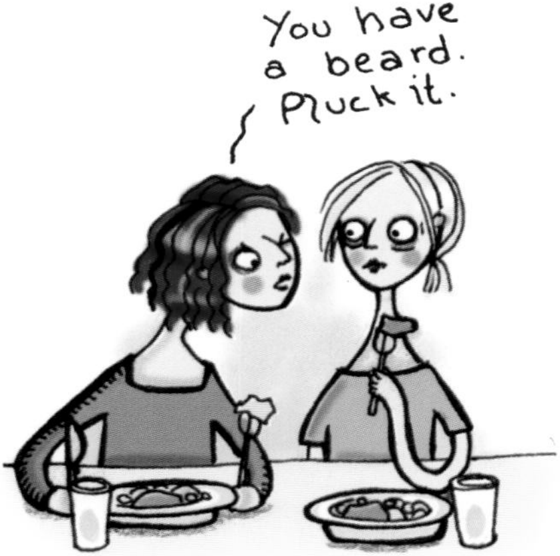
You have a beard. Pluck it.

in all areas.

Younger sister: You were always my best personal lab rat.

Older sister: You were always my best personal bodyguard.

Younger sister: You always let me in through the window at night when I was supposed to be grounded.

You should so thank me !

Older sister; You exhausted
our parents so that I got
to be even wilder, younger.

Older sister: You supplied me
with a free taxi service.

Younger sister: You supplied me
with a free taxi service.

When we are old, I will have a partner in crime.

No matter how much we argue,
you will never go away,
because we are family.

You actually know what I
want for my birthday . . .

and at Christmas I can swap
unwanted presents with you.

The only time you look down
on me is when you're picking
me up from the floor.

You bring me back down to earth when necessary.

In your eyes, I will
always be perfect.

Between the two of us,
someone is bound to remember
our relatives' birthdays.

Through you I get to
meet more friends.

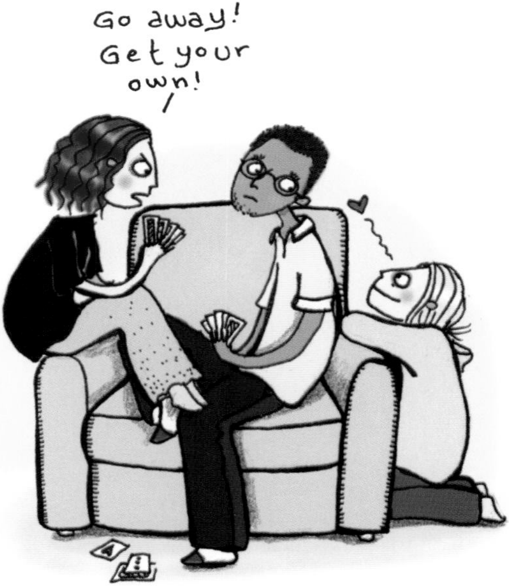
Go away! Get your own!

Through you I get to

meet more men.

You tell me when I need a makeover, and then help me achieve one.

You keep my friends entertained
for hours with amusing stories
of my childhood.

Wherever I am out in the world, I am never alone.

You love me for who
you can be when
you are with me.